DOUBLE ENTRY JOURNAL

CORNERSTONE

Building on Your Best

SECOND EDITION

RHONDA J. MONTGOMERY
The University of Nevada, Las Vegas

PATRICIA G. MOODY
The University of South Carolina

ROBERT M. SHERFIELD
The Community College of Southern Nevada

D1366942

Prentice Hall
Upper Saddle River, New Jersey 07458

©2000 Prentice-Hall, Inc.
Upper Saddle River, NJ 07458

10 9 8 7 6 5 4 3 2 1

ISBN 0-205-30654-3

Printed in the United States of America

"There are two powers in the world,

the sword and the pen;

and in the end,

the former is always conquered

by the latter."

Napoleon

To Our Students:

This supplement is provided to you as a means of communication with your professor and/or peers. As you work through the text and use this journal, we ask that you explore new thoughts, write honestly, take chances and develop your ideas fully. Each professor will use this journal differently. Some will require you to write daily, some will ask you to for weekly submissions and others may ask you to write only one entry per chapter. In all of these situations, the success of this journal is dependent on YOU.

There are sixteen chapters in the book and each chapter is represented by three entries. **The first** entry asks you to explore your feelings related to the chapter exercise, *"At This Moment."* **The second** entry is a *One Minute Journal* activity. In one minute or less, jot down the major ideas that you learned from the chapter. **The third** entry for each chapter is an *Internet Activity* provided to help you explore sites related to chapter content.

Enjoy your journey. If you use this supplement wisely, you will begin to learn things about yourself, your peers and your professors. Most importantly, you will be creating a history of your first year that will last a lifetime.

Happy writing,

Rhonda, Pat and Robb

CHAPTER 1
Preparing for and Dealing With Change
Entry One
Response To: AT THIS MOMENT
from Page 05 of Cornerstone

Student Entry   **Instructor Entry**

Student Entry

Instructor Entry

CHAPTER 1
Preparing for and Dealing With Change
Entry Two
THE ONE MINUTE JOURNAL
In one minute or less, jot down the major ideas learned in Chapter 1

Student Entry   **Instructor Entry**

Student Entry

Instructor Entry

CHAPTER 1
Preparing for and Dealing With Change
Entry Three
Response To: ONLINE STUDY GUIDE
Log onto http://www.prenhall.com/montgomery
Click on First Year Orientation
Click on Cornerstone Online Study Guide
Choose one DESTINATION site, explore it and respond to your findings

Student Entry	Instructor Entry

Student Entry   **Instructor Entry**

Student Entry	Instructor Entry

Student Entry　　　　　　　　　　**Instructor Entry**

CHAPTER 2
Motivation, Goal Setting and Self-Esteem
Entry Two
THE ONE MINUTE JOURNAL
In one minute or less, jot down the major ideas learned in Chapter 2

Student Entry   **Instructor Entry**

Student Entry

Instructor Entry

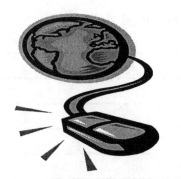

CHAPTER 2
Motivation, Goal Setting and Self-Esteem
Entry Three
Response To: ONLINE STUDY GUIDE
Log onto http://www.prenhall.com/montgomery
Click on First Year Orientation
Click on Cornerstone Online Study Guide
Choose one DESTINATION site, explore it and respond to your findings

Student Entry	Instructor Entry

Student Entry   **Instructor Entry**

Student Entry	Instructor Entry

Student Entry   **Instructor Entry**

CHAPTER 3
Learning Through Multiple Intelligences
Entry Two
THE ONE MINUTE JOURNAL
**In one minute or less, jot down
the major ideas learned in Chapter 3**

Student Entry   **Instructor Entry**

Student Entry   **Instructor Entry**

CHAPTER 3
Learning Through Multiple Intelligences
Entry Three
Response To: ONLINE STUDY GUIDE
Log onto http://www.prehnall.com/montgomery
Click on First Year Orientation
Click on Cornerstone Online Study Guide
Choose one DESTINATION site, explore it and respond to your findings

Student Entry   **Instructor Entry**

Student Entry   **Instructor Entry**

Student Entry	Instructor Entry

Student Entry   **Instructor Entry**

CHAPTER 4
Using Critical Thinking Skills
Entry Two
THE ONE MINUTE JOURNAL
In one minute or less, jot down
the major ideas learned in Chapter 4

Student Entry   **Instructor Entry**

Student Entry

Instructor Entry

CHAPTER 4
Using Critical Thinking Skills
Entry Three
Response To: ONLINE STUDY GUIDE
Log onto http://www.prenhall.com/montgomery
Click on First Year Orientation
Click on Cornerstone Online Study Guide
Choose one DESTINATION site, explore it and respond to your findings

Student Entry	Instructor Entry

Student Entry   **Instructor Entry**

Student Entry   **Instructor Entry**

_____|_____
_____|_____
_____|_____
_____|_____
_____|_____
_____|_____
_____|_____
_____|_____
_____|_____
_____|_____
_____|_____
_____|_____
_____|_____
_____|_____
_____|_____
_____|_____
_____|_____
_____|_____
_____|_____
_____|_____
_____|_____
_____|_____

Student Entry   **Instructor Entry**

CHAPTER 5
Priority Management
Entry Two
THE ONE MINUTE JOURNAL
In one minute or less, jot down
the major ideas learned in Chapter 5

Student Entry   **Instructor Entry**

Student Entry   **Instructor Entry**

CHAPTER 5
Priority Management
Entry Three
Response To: ONLINE STUDY GUIDE
Log onto http://www.prehnall.com/montgomery
Click on First Year Orientation
Click on Cornerstone Online Study Guide
Choose one DESTINATION site, explore it and respond to your findings

Student Entry	Instructor Entry

Student Entry   **Instructor Entry**

Student Entry	Instructor Entry

Student Entry　　　　　　　　　　**Instructor Entry**

CHAPTER 6
The Art of Active Listening
Entry Two
THE ONE MINUTE JOURNAL
In one minute or less, jot down
the major ideas learned in Chapter 6

Student Entry   **Instructor Entry**

Student Entry   **Instructor Entry**

CHAPTER 6
The Art of Active Listening
Entry Three
Response To: ONLINE STUDY GUIDE
Log onto http://www.prenhall.com/montgomery
Click on First Year Orientation
Click on Cornerstone Online Study Guide
Choose one DESTINATION site, explore it and respond to your findings

Student Entry	Instructor Entry

Student Entry   **Instructor Entry**

Student Entry

Instructor Entry

Student Entry   **Instructor Entry**

CHAPTER 7
The Essentials of Note Taking
Entry Two
THE ONE MINUTE JOURNAL
In one minute or less, jot down
the major ideas learned in Chapter 7

Student Entry   **Instructor Entry**

Student Entry   **Instructor Entry**

CHAPTER 7
The Essentials of Note Taking
Entry Three
Response To: ONLINE STUDY GUIDE
Log onto http://www.prehnall.com/montgomery
Click on First Year Orientation
Click on Cornerstone Online Study Guide
Choose one DESTINATION site, explore it and respond to your findings

Student Entry   **Instructor Entry**

Student Entry   **Instructor Entry**

Student Entry	Instructor Entry

Student Entry

Instructor Entry

CHAPTER 8
Studying for Success
Entry Two
THE ONE MINUTE JOURNAL
In one minute or less, jot down
the major ideas learned in Chapter 8

Student Entry   **Instructor Entry**

Student Entry

Instructor Entry

CHAPTER 8
Studying for Success
Entry Three
Response To: ONLINE STUDY GUIDE
Log onto http://www.prenhall.com/montgomery
Click on First Year Orientation
Click on Cornerstone Online Study Guide
Choose one DESTINATION site, explore it and respond to your findings

Student Entry   **Instructor Entry**

Student Entry　　　　　　　　**Instructor Entry**

Student Entry | **Instructor Entry**

_____ | _____
_____ | _____
_____ | _____
_____ | _____
_____ | _____
_____ | _____
_____ | _____
_____ | _____
_____ | _____
_____ | _____
_____ | _____
_____ | _____
_____ | _____
_____ | _____
_____ | _____
_____ | _____
_____ | _____
_____ | _____
_____ | _____
_____ | _____
_____ | _____

Student Entry

Instructor Entry

CHAPTER 9
Strategies for Test Taking
Entry Two
THE ONE MINUTE JOURNAL
In one minute or less, jot down
the major ideas learned in Chapter 9

Student Entry   **Instructor Entry**

_____|_____
_____|_____
_____|_____
_____|_____
_____|_____
_____|_____
_____|_____
_____|_____
_____|_____
_____|_____
_____|_____
_____|_____
_____|_____
_____|_____
_____|_____
_____|_____
_____|_____
_____|_____
_____|_____
_____|_____
_____|_____

Student Entry   **Instructor Entry**

CHAPTER 9
Strategies for Test Taking
Entry Three
Response To: ONLINE STUDY GUIDE
Log onto http://www.prenhall.com/montgomery
Click on First Year Orientation
Click on Cornerstone Online Study Guide
Choose one DESTINATION site, explore it and respond to your findings

Student Entry   **Instructor Entry**

Student Entry   **Instructor Entry**

CHAPTER 10
Writing and Public Speaking
Entry One
Response To: AT THIS MOMENT
from Page 224 of Cornerstone

Student Entry   **Instructor Entry**

_____
_____
_____
_____
_____
_____
_____
_____
_____
_____
_____
_____
_____
_____
_____
_____
_____
_____
_____
_____
_____
_____
_____
_____

Student Entry

Instructor Entry

CHAPTER 10
Writing and Public Speaking
Entry Two
THE ONE MINUTE JOURNAL
In one minute or less, jot down
the major ideas learned in Chapter 10

Student Entry   **Instructor Entry**

_____|_____
_____|_____
_____|_____
_____|_____
_____|_____
_____|_____
_____|_____
_____|_____
_____|_____
_____|_____
_____|_____
_____|_____
_____|_____
_____|_____
_____|_____
_____|_____
_____|_____
_____|_____
_____|_____
_____|_____
_____|_____

Student Entry   **Instructor Entry**

CHAPTER 10
Writing and Public Speaking
Entry Three
Response To: ONLINE STUDY GUIDE
Log onto http://www.prenhall.com/montgomery
Click on First Year Orientation
Click on Cornerstone Online Study Guide
Choose one DESTINATION site, explore it and respond to your findings

Student Entry   **Instructor Entry**

Student Entry   **Instructor Entry**

Student Entry   **Instructor Entry**

Student Entry

Instructor Entry

CHAPTER 11
The Power of Relationships
Entry Two
THE ONE MINUTE JOURNAL
In one minute or less, jot down the major ideas learned in Chapter 11

Student Entry   **Instructor Entry**

Student Entry　　　　　　　　**Instructor Entry**

CHAPTER 11
The Power of Relationships
Entry Three
Response To: ONLINE STUDY GUIDE
Log onto http://www.prenhall.com/montgomery
Click on First Year Orientation
Click on Cornerstone Online Study Guide
Choose one DESTINATION site, explore it and respond to your findings

Student Entry	Instructor Entry

Student Entry

Instructor Entry

Student Entry   **Instructor Entry**

Student Entry   **Instructor Entry**

CHAPTER 12
Celebrating Diversity
Entry Two
THE ONE MINUTE JOURNAL
**In one minute or less, jot down
the major ideas learned in Chapter 12**

Student Entry   **Instructor Entry**

Student Entry   **Instructor Entry**

Celebrating Diversity
Entry Three
Response To: ONLINE STUDY GUIDE
Log onto http://www.prenhall.com/montgomery
Click on First Year Orientation
Click on Cornerstone Online Study Guide
Choose one DESTINATION site, explore it and respond to your findings

Student Entry   **Instructor Entry**

Student Entry   **Instructor Entry**

Student Entry   **Instructor Entry**

_____

_____

_____

_____

_____

_____

_____

_____

_____

_____

_____

_____

_____

_____

_____

_____

_____

_____

_____

_____

_____

_____

_____

Student Entry　　　　　　　　**Instructor Entry**

CHAPTER 13
A Plan for Wellness
Entry Two
THE ONE MINUTE JOURNAL
In one minute or less, jot down
the major ideas learned in Chapter 13

Student Entry   **Instructor Entry**

Student Entry   **Instructor Entry**

CHAPTER 13
A Plan for Wellness
Entry Three
Response To: ONLINE STUDY GUIDE
Log onto http://www.prenhall.com/montgomery
Click on First Year Orientation
Click on Cornerstone Online Study Guide
Choose one DESTINATION site, explore it and respond to your findings

Student Entry   **Instructor Entry**

Student Entry

Instructor Entry

Student Entry   **Instructor Entry**

Student Entry   **Instructor Entry**

CHAPTER 14
Controlling Stress
Entry Two
THE ONE MINUTE JOURNAL
In one minute or less, jot down
the major ideas learned in Chapter 14

Student Entry   **Instructor Entry**

Student Entry   **Instructor Entry**

CHAPTER 14
Controlling Stress
Entry Three
Response To: ONLINE STUDY GUIDE
Log onto http://www.prenhall.com/montgomery
Click on First Year Orientation
Click on Cornerstone Online Study Guide
Choose one DESTINATION site, explore it and respond to your findings

Student Entry	Instructor Entry

Student Entry

Instructor Entry

Student Entry   **Instructor Entry**

Student Entry   **Instructor Entry**

CHAPTER 15
Social and Personal Responsibility
Entry Two
THE ONE MINUTE JOURNAL
In one minute or less, jot down
the major ideas learned in Chapter 15

Student Entry   **Instructor Entry**

_____ | _____
_____ | _____
_____ | _____
_____ | _____
_____ | _____
_____ | _____
_____ | _____
_____ | _____
_____ | _____
_____ | _____
_____ | _____
_____ | _____
_____ | _____
_____ | _____
_____ | _____
_____ | _____
_____ | _____
_____ | _____
_____ | _____
_____ | _____
_____ | _____
_____ | _____

Student Entry   **Instructor Entry**

CHAPTER 15
Social and Personal Responsibility
Entry Three
Response To: ONLINE STUDY GUIDE
Log onto http://www.prenhall.com/montgomery
Click on First Year Orientation
Click on Cornerstone Online Study Guide
Choose one DESTINATION site, explore it and respond to your findings

Student Entry	Instructor Entry

Student Entry   **Instructor Entry**

CHAPTER 16
Career Planning
Entry One
Response To: AT THIS MOMENT
from Page 363 of Cornerstone

Student Entry   **Instructor Entry**

Student Entry

Instructor Entry

CHAPTER 16
Career Planning
Entry Two
THE ONE MINUTE JOURNAL
In one minute or less, jot down
the major ideas learned in Chapter 16

Student Entry   **Instructor Entry**

Student Entry   **Instructor Entry**

CHAPTER 16
Career Planning
Entry Three
Response To: ONLINE STUDY GUIDE
Log onto http://www.prenhal.com/montgomery
Click on First Year Orientation
Click on Cornerstone Online Study Guide
Choose one DESTINATION site, explore it and respond to your findings

Student Entry   **Instructor Entry**

Student Entry   **Instructor Entry**